EXPLORING THE
SUBATOMIC WORLD

Understanding
ELECTRONS

B. H. Fields and
Fred Bortz

Cavendish
Square

New York

To Elon, for the electricity he brings to life.

Published in 2016 by Cavendish Square Publishing, LLC
243 5th Avenue, Suite 136, New York, NY 10016

Library of Congress Cataloging-in-Publication Data

Bortz, Fred.
Understanding electrons / by Fred Bortz and B.H. Fields.
p. cm. — (Exploring the subatomic world)
Includes index.
ISBN 978-1-50260-538-2 (hardcover) ISBN 978-1-50260-539-9 (ebook)
1. Electrons — Juvenile literature. I. Bortz, Fred, 1944-. II. Title.
QC793.5.E62 B67 2016
539.7'2112—d23

Editorial Director: David McNamara
Editor: Andrew Coddington
Copy Editor: Cynthia Roby
Art Director: Jeffrey Talbot
Designer: Stephanie Flecha
Senior Production Manager: Jennifer Ryder-Talbot
Production Editor: Renni Johnson
Photo Research: J8 Media

Printed in the United States of America

Contents

Introduction

What would modern life be like without **electronics**? We live surrounded by devices. We connect to each other through computers and the Internet. We use pocket-sized cellular phones to communicate by voice, text, pictures, or video. We watch and listen to news, opinions, music, and entertainment on radio, television, and streaming audio and video. We can cook with microwaves instead of gas or electricity. We have global positioning system (GPS) receivers small enough to hold in one hand or mount on car windshields. Their programs and detailed maps tell us where we are in the world and how to get to our destination. Robots with electronic controls work in factories, hospitals, and even on other planets.

All of that technology has grown from our understanding of electrons, which are among the lightest bits of matter known to science. We can trace that very modern understanding back to a very ancient question. About 2,500 years ago, Greek philosopher Democritus and his mentor, Leucippus, asked, "What is matter made of?"

Democritus and Leucippus imagined cutting a piece of matter in half, then cutting one of its halves in half, then cutting one of those pieces in half, and so on until the resulting pieces could no longer be cut. The last pieces would be indivisible, or *atomos* in Greek. Democritus's **atoms** turned out to be similar to what we call **molecules** today. A water molecule—two hydrogen atoms combined with one oxygen atom—is not indivisible, but it is the smallest speck of matter that can still be called water.

Hydrogen and oxygen are examples of substances that scientists call **elements**. In a pure element, all the atoms are the same. Scientists classify water as a **compound**, a substance with more than one kind of atom, but with all its atoms combined into the same kind of molecules. The science of chemistry deals with the way atoms and molecules interact, react, and combine.

If molecules can be divided into atoms, it is natural to ask if atoms can also be divided. And if so, might we look into the atom to understand why only certain combinations of atoms form molecules. A little more than a century ago, physicists began to answer those questions. As they probed inside atoms, they found a deeper understanding of not only the chemical behavior of matter, but also other phenomena such as electricity, magnetism, and light.

This book contains the story of the first subatomic particle to be discovered (the electron) and explores the knowledge and technological advances that people have gained from studying it.

1 DISCOVERING
the Electron

Our story begins at the world-famous Cavendish Laboratory at Britain's Cambridge University. A twenty-four-year-old scientist named Joseph John "J. J." Thomson (1856–1940) arrived there in 1881, and he found that the atmosphere there was "electric" in more ways than one. The laboratory's founder, James Clerk Maxwell (1831–1879), was famous for formulating a set of four equations that described the relationship between electricity, magnetism, and light waves. Thomson hoped to follow in his footsteps.

Other major discoveries of that time came from chemistry. By studying the reactions between different substances, chemists had concluded that matter was composed of atoms, and that atoms combined in particular ways to form molecules. They thought those atoms were indivisible. They also had discovered that electricity was related to chemical reactions. But where the electrical nature of matter came from remained a mystery.

Cathode Ray Experiments

Young Thomson wanted to use his mathematical gifts to make discoveries about the electrical nature of matter just as Maxwell had done for the electromagnetic nature of light. But his boss, John William Strutt (1842–1919), more commonly called Lord Rayleigh, who became Cavendish Professor in 1879 after Maxwell's death, had other plans. Rayleigh believed that in physics, mathematical skills should not stand alone. If Thomson intended to work at the Cavendish, he would have to do more than calculation. He would have to work in the laboratory!

Unfortunately, Thomson was not very skilled with scientific apparatus. His contributions to experiments were more of the mind than of the hand. "J. J. was very awkward with his fingers, and I found it very necessary not to encourage him to handle the instruments!" said H. F. Newall (1857–1944), Thomson's assistant in his early years at the lab. "But he was very helpful in talking over the ways in which he thought things ought to go."

Thomson's most important investigations were into the well-known but poorly understood phenomenon of **cathode rays**. The cathode ray tubes Thomson

Joseph John (J. J.) Thomson's work with cathode rays led him to discover the electron in 1897.

Particles or Waves?

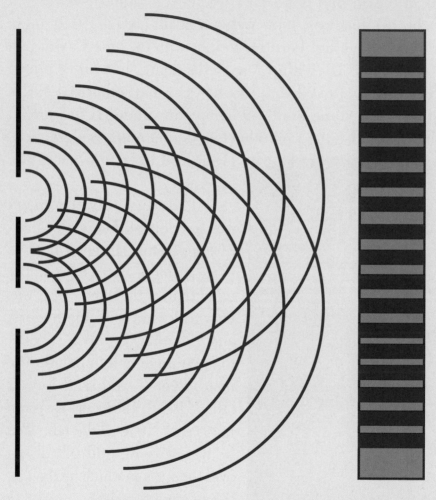

Answering a great question in a famous 1801 experiment, Thomas Young produced an interference pattern of light and dark bands that demonstrated the wave nature of light.

In the history of science, one of the great questions has been about the nature of light. It first came to prominence in the seventeenth century, when two great thinkers came to opposite conclusions. England's Sir Isaac Newton (1648–1727) was convinced that light was a stream of particles, while Christiaan Huygens (1629–1695) of the Netherlands was just as certain it was made of waves.

Without evidence to support one view or the other, scientists argued about it for more than one hundred years. Finally in 1801, Thomas Young (1773–1829) settled the question with an experiment. He passed light through two closely spaced pinholes in front of a white screen. Instead of seeing two bright spots as he would expect if the light was a stream of particles, Young observed a pattern of dark and light bands called an interference pattern that would be expected if two waves met. At places on the screen where two wave crests met, it was bright. At other places, wave crests met valleys and cancelled out, producing darkness.

It seemed that the argument was settled in favor of Huygens—though you will read later that it wasn't as settled as scientists thought. At the Cavendish, J. J. Thomson would revisit the wave-or-particle question for a phenomenon called cathode rays. And his findings would turn out to be just as dramatic and important as Young's and Maxwell's were for light.

J. J. Thomson's Cathode Ray Tube. The development of better vacuum pumps enabled J. J. Thomson to use this apparatus to determine that cathode rays were streams of negatively charged particles, which today we know are electrons.

used were primitive versions of those used in old-fashioned television picture tubes. As early as the 1830s, scientists were experimenting with the electrical behavior of gases in glass tubes with two electrodes inserted at opposite ends. They needed low pressures for their experiments, so they pumped hard on the tubes to draw out most of the gas before sealing them. The invention in 1855 of a better vacuum pump made it possible to remove nearly all the gas, and things began to get very interesting when electricity was applied. The remaining gas would glow, especially near the negative electrode, or **cathode**.

When Thomson began studying cathode rays, scientists knew that the cathode was shooting out tiny, negatively charged particles. But they were divided about whether the particles themselves were the cathode rays, or whether the glow resulted from waves that the particles produced. Thomson hoped to settle the question with an experiment.

As you read in "Particles or Waves," the question of whether cathode rays were waves or particles echoed a similar question about light. A famous 1801 experiment performed by Thomas Young seemed to settle the question in favor of light waves. And that view became even stronger in 1861–62 when Maxwell published his four famous equations. Those equations predicted waves of electromagnetic energy that travel through space at the speed of light.

For cathode rays, however, there were no equations like Maxwell's, and so far, experimental results had been mixed. So Thomson kept an open mind and began by repeating what others had done.

He applied magnetic fields to the tubes, and the rays curved in the direction that the magnetic field would cause negatively charged particles to curve. But when he passed the beam between a pair of oppositely charged electrified plates, the cathode rays went straight through, producing a glowing spot on the center of the glass. If cathode rays were streams of negative particles, the glowing spot on the glass should have been offset in the direction of the positively charged plate—but it wasn't.

Maxwell's Equations and Electromagnetic Waves

Although you need to know calculus to understand the mathematics of Maxwell's equations, it is fairly easy to understand the phenomena that they describe. One phenomenon is the force between two electric charges. In a famous experiment in 1785, Charles-Augustin de Coulomb (1736–1806) measured how that force depends on the size of the two charges and their separation. He discovered that the force behaved in the same way as the gravity between two bodies, except that it can be either attractive (if the charges are of opposite sign) or repulsive (if the charges have the same sign).

That relationship is a formula known as Coulomb's Law and contains a natural constant that is needed to relate the units used to measure force (such as pounds or newtons) to the charges (measured in coulombs) and the separation (measured in feet, meters, or centimeters). Scientists call that constant ε_0 (epsilon sub-zero, where the zero means the charges have no material between them). A similar equation relates the force between two magnetic poles and contains a constant μ_0 (mu sub-zero).

The other two phenomena relate electricity to magnetism. The best-known experimenter in that area was Michael Faraday (1791–1867) in the 1820s and early 1830s. Faraday discovered that electric coils can produce a magnetic field and that a changing

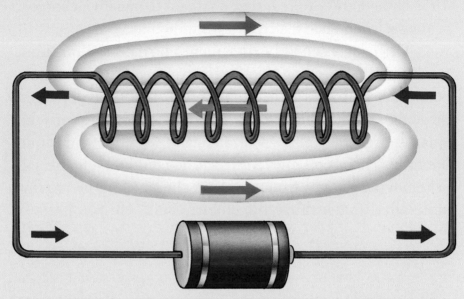

A simple electromagnet. A battery connected to a coil of wire produces an electric current (shown by the red arrows) and causes the coil to act like a bar magnet. The blue lines and arrows show the direction that a compass needle would point when placed in or near the coil.

magnetic field can generate an electric current. His principles are still used today in electric generators and motors.

When the equations are combined, they predict the possibility of **electromagnetic waves**, whose speed can be calculated from ε_0 and μ_0. Astonishingly, the calculated speed of those waves turns out to match the measured speed of light.

Thomson then devised three new experiments. In the first, he put an **electrometer,** a device that measures electrical charge, into the tube. When the glow struck the electrometer, the device indicated a large negative charge. When the glow just missed, the electrometer measured very little charge. Thus cathode rays were either a stream of negative charges, or they carried such a stream with them.

Thomson's second experiment clarified the puzzling results with the electrified plates. He reasoned that an energetic beam of negative particles would electrify the gas it passed through, and the charged gas atoms would drift toward the oppositely charged plate, neutralizing the electric field within the tube. Thomson believed that if he could do a better job of removing the gas from the tube, there would be too few molecules to neutralize the electric field. He got the best

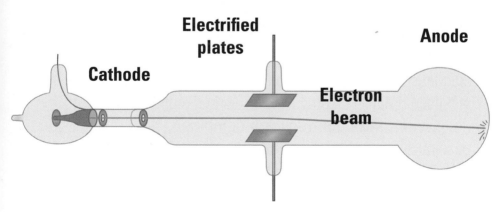

Thomson's Second Experiment. Using an improved vacuum pump, J. J. Thomson repeated earlier experiments that had not produced clear results. With almost no gas left in the tube, the cathode rays curved toward the positively charged plate (the lower plate in this diagram), demonstrating that they were negatively charged particles.

available vacuum pump and repeated the experiment. Sure enough, the cathode rays now deflected toward the positive plate. Thomson was now confident that they were negatively charged "corpuscles," that is, particles shot from the cathode.

The second experiment also enabled Thomson to measure the speed of those tiny particles. He added a magnet to the apparatus. The magnetic force on the corpuscles depended on their speed, but the electrical force did not. Thomson arranged the fields so that the magnetic and electrical forces were in opposite directions, and then adjusted the fields until the particles went straight, indicating that the forces were equal. Knowing that, he was able to compute the speed from the strength of the two fields.

Thomson was then was ready for a final experiment that would allow him to compute the corpuscles' electric charge compared to their mass. He allowed just enough gas back into a tube so that the cathode rays' glowing path could be seen and measured precisely. He applied a magnetic field and measured the curvature of the path. Knowing the speed, the curvature, and the formula for magnetic force, he was able to use his results to measure the charge-to-mass ratio of the corpuscles.

He discovered that the charge to mass ratio was about one thousand times as large for these corpuscles as for an electrically charged hydrogen atom, the lightest particle known at that time. For that to be true, the corpuscles either had to carry a lot of charge or have very little mass. Other scientists' measurements

Hydrogen nucleus   **Electron**

$$\frac{1}{1} = \frac{\text{(hydrogen nucleus)}}{\quad}$$ $$\frac{1}{1,000} = \frac{\text{(electron)}}{\quad}$$

Thomson's third experiment measured the charge-to-mass ratio of the "corpuscles" in cathode rays. The corpuscles carried the same amount of charge in less than a thousandth of the mass of a positively charged hydrogen atom. More precise measurements have since revealed a ratio of approximately 1,837-to-1.

indicated that there was a basic minimum unit of electric charge for both positive and negative electricity, so Thomson assumed that each negative corpuscle and each positive hydrogen atom carried the same amount of electrical charge. That meant that the corpuscle had only a thousandth of the mass of the tiny hydrogen atom. Today, we know more precisely that this particle's mass is only 1/1,837.15 of the hydrogen atom.

The result was astounding. Cathode rays were beams of particles, as Thomson had suspected all along, but their mass was far smaller than he could have imagined. In his 1906 Nobel Prize lecture, Thomson still called the particles "corpuscles." But he realized their importance went far beyond cathode rays, stating, "The corpuscle appears to form a part of all kinds of matter under the most diverse conditions; it seems natural therefore to regard it as one of the bricks of which atoms are built up."

In other words, Thomson was stating that his corpuscles were subatomic particles. It was not long before people began calling them electrons. The door to the subatomic world had opened.

2 ELECTRICITY
and Magnetism, Matter and Light

Thomson's work answered some questions, but as is often true in science, it raised many more. Atoms contain tiny, negatively charged electrons, but they are electrically neutral. That means they must contain other subatomic particles that carry a positive electric charge. Scientists wondered how electrons and those other subatomic particles fit together to make different kinds of atoms. And how, they asked, do those subatomic parts relate to the rules of nature that govern the way atoms combine to form molecules?

Discovering the Nucleus

J. J. Thomson put forward an educated guess about the internal structure of atoms. Since electrons carry so little mass, he envisioned the positively charged bulk of atoms as a kind of pudding containing tiny electron plums.

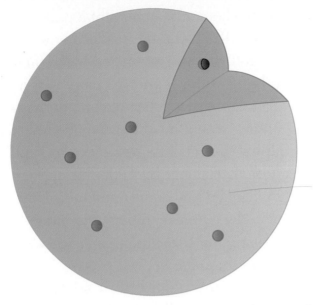

After discovering that atoms have tiny, negatively charged electrons, Thomson wondered about their structure. He proposed a "plum pudding" model where a positively charged bulk, containing most of the mass, was the pudding and the electrons were the small "plums."

Though Thomson's plum pudding model seemed sensible, no one tested it until Ernest Rutherford (1871–1937) came up with a way to probe matter with radioactive beams. Born in New Zealand in 1871, Rutherford first explored radioactivity as Thomson's student in the Cavendish Laboratory between 1895 and 1898. He quickly discovered two distinct forms of radioactivity and named them "alpha rays" and "beta rays" after the first two letters of the Greek alphabet.

When Rutherford finished his work at Cambridge, he took a faculty position at McGill University in Montreal, Canada, where he and student Frederick Soddy (1877–1956) discovered "gamma rays," a third form of radioactivity, in 1902. They also discovered that alpha and beta radiation were streams of fast-moving particles of opposite electric charge. The alphas were positively charged and much more massive than the negatively charged betas. (We now know that beta rays are electrons.) Rutherford returned to England in 1907 as a professor at the University of Manchester full of ideas about how to apply his discoveries.

Rutherford planned to shoot a beam of alpha particles through a thin sheet of metallic foil and measure how the alphas deflected, or scattered, as they interacted with atoms in the metal foil. By studying alpha scattering carefully, he hoped to be able to determine the size, spacing, and perhaps even the shape of the atoms in the foil. First, he needed to know more about the alpha "bullets" he was shooting, and he needed ways to keep track of them. By 1908, his student Hans Geiger (1882–1945) had devised an instrument to detect and count alpha particles. The two researchers then quickly confirmed Rutherford's suspicion that alpha particles were helium atoms without their electrons.

The next year, 1909, they began their scattering experiments. Would the plum pudding model be proven correct, or would they find, as some people expected, evidence that atoms were hard little balls? Nearly all the alphas passed straight through the foil or were deflected only slightly. If

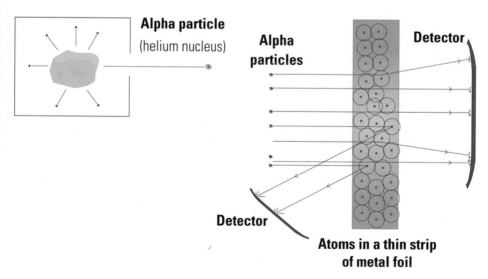

Ernest Rutherford discovered the atomic nucleus by directing a stream of alpha particles at a thin metal foil and measuring how the alpha particles scattered. Most of the alphas passed straight through or deflected only slightly. But to his great surprise, a few deflected far off to the side or even bounced backward. That indicated that the atoms were mostly empty space with most of their mass and positive charge concentrated in a very tiny central region.

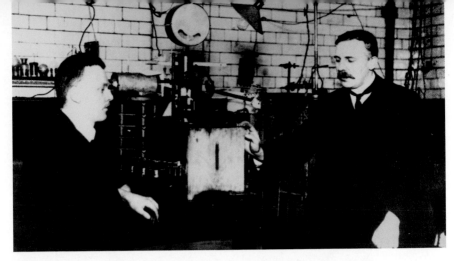

Rutherford with his student Hans Geiger (left), who built the detectors that led to the discovery of the nucleus.

the atoms were hard balls, Rutherford and Geiger would have expected more deflection. It was beginning to look as if Thomson's model was correct, but the researchers needed more detailed measurements to be certain.

Rutherford also needed to clarify one puzzling result. A few alpha particles were unaccounted for. He wondered if the missing particles had been deflected so much that they missed the detectors. If so, what was scattering those few alphas through such large angles while most passed nearly straight through the foil?

Always intrigued by unlikely results, but not wanting to divert Geiger from his detailed measurements, Rutherford assigned the task of looking for large-angle scattering to Ernest Marsden (1889–1970), a young student just learning the techniques of research. Marsden found the missing alpha particles, and a great surprise. Those alpha particles scattered to the left or right of the original detectors, and a few even scattered backward! Rutherford described this result as "almost as incredible as if you had fired a 15-inch [38.1-centimeter] shell at a piece of tissue paper and it came back and hit you." Rutherford

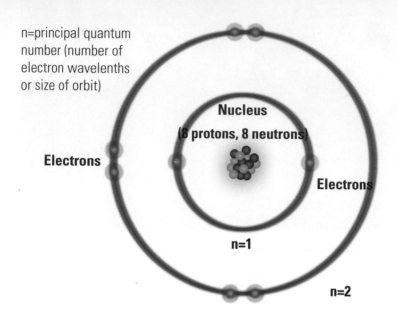

n=principal quantum number (number of electron wavelenths or size of orbit)

Nucleus
(8 protons, 8 neutrons)

Electrons

Electrons

n=1

n=2

Rutherford described the atom as a miniature solar system, mostly empty space with electrons orbiting the nucleus. Electrical attraction plays the role of gravity. That model raised some questions that were later resolved by replacing orbits with shells containing certain numbers of electrons, such as in this modern depiction of an oxygen atom.

published his findings in 1911, explaining his results with a new model of the atom.

In Rutherford's model, an atom was like a miniature solar system with electrical forces playing the role of gravity. The atom is mostly empty space and most of its mass is concentrated in a very small, positively charged central body called the nucleus. In orbit around that minuscule sun are much tinier negatively charged "planets," the electrons.

This model made sense of both Geiger's and Marsden's results. Because atoms are mostly empty space, most alpha particles passed through the foil without coming very close to a nucleus, and thus scattered very little. On rare occasions, a fast-moving alpha particle made a nearly direct hit on a nucleus, which in the metals Rutherford used was much more massive than the alpha, and it scattered the alpha sideways or even backward.

Secrets in the Spectrum

Rutherford's model opened up new questions. According to Maxwell's equations, an electrically charged body moving along a curve must radiate energy in the form of electromagnetic waves. Thus orbiting electrons in atoms should be constantly glowing and losing energy, and that would cause them to spiral inward toward the nucleus. It wouldn't be long before the nucleus consumed its electron planets altogether. If the planetary model was correct, then the laws of **electromagnetism**, or the laws of motion—or both—must be wrong, at least when they are examined on the atomic scale.

The research that would resolve this problem had, in fact, already been done, and had produced equally puzzling results. In 1895, the renowned Professor Max Planck (1858–1947) at the University of Berlin in Germany had just turned his theoretical skills to a new problem. Could he come up with a formula that described the **spectrum**—the different colors of light—that radiated from hot bodies?

Planck had plenty of experimental data with which he could work. Scientists heated furnaces and observed the light that came from holes in their sides. Using a spectrometer, a device that spreads light into its component colors like a prism, they had produced graphs showing the brightness of each color in the glow. On the graph, each color represented a corresponding frequency, or the rate at which the electromagnetic wave wiggles. For visible light, red has the lowest frequency and violet has the highest. The measurements went from infrared (below red) through ultraviolet (above violet) at higher temperatures.

At all temperatures, the graphs had a common appearance. Going from infrared to ultraviolet, they would rise to a peak

Atoms as Solar Systems

Rutherford's discovery led him to propose a new picture of the atom. An atom is neither a little hard ball, as some people thought, nor like positively charged pudding with tiny negatively charged electron plums, as J. J. Thomson had surmised. Marsden's experiments showed the atom as more of a solar system held together by electric forces.

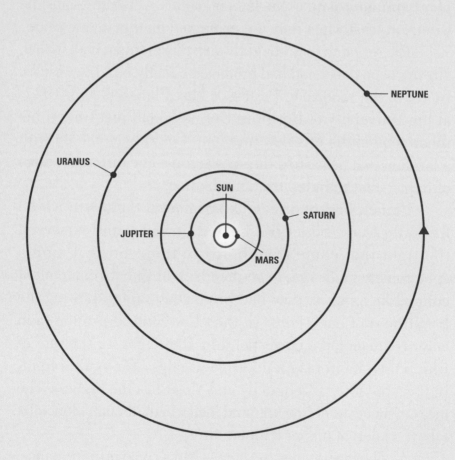

But how far does that similarity go? In the solar system, the sun's mass is about one thousand times as much as all the planets, moons, asteroids, comets, and other orbiting objects combined. In the lightest atom, hydrogen, the nucleus is about two thousand times as heavy as its one orbiting electron. In heavier atoms, the nucleus can have more than five thousand times the mass of all its electrons combined. Physicists would say those mass ratios are of the same "order of magnitude," since they are within a factor of ten of each other.

But what about the size of the atom compared to its nucleus? Marsden's experiment with gold foil showed that a gold atom is at least three thousand times as large as its nucleus. Today we know the actual number is about thirty thousand. The most distant of the icy objects in the Kuiper Belt, which includes Pluto, have orbits that carry them as far away from the sun as about ten thousand times the sun's diameter. Again, those ratios have the same order of magnitude. So we could say that Rutherford's picture of the atom, as a solar system with a heavier sun and more distant planets, is a reasonable way to think of it.

Even so, Rutherford and others saw serious problems with that picture. Those would not be resolved until the development of a new branch of physics called **quantum mechanics**.

Rutherford's model of an atom is similar to the solar system, but with differences in size and mass. This diagram shows the sun and the orbits of the five outermost major planets (drawn approximately to scale). The dwarf planet Pluto in the Kuiper Belt (not shown here) follows an orbit that takes it about twice as far from the sun as Neptune. If an atom were enlarged so that its nucleus was as large as the sun, the orbits of the electrons would go about ten times as far away as Pluto. The mass of the sun is about one thousand times as much as everything that orbits it, while the mass of the nucleus of a heavy atom is typically five thousand times as much as all its electrons.

The work of Niels Bohr (left) and Max Planck (right) opened the doors to quantum mechanics. In 1900, Planck invented the light quantum as a mathematical device to explain the spectrum of glowing bodies. To his surprise, it turned out to have physical meaning as well. Bohr found that the quantum also explained the line spectrum of gases if the electrons occupied a particular set of orbits around the nucleus.

and then drop off to zero. Higher temperatures produced more intense light, so the peaks of the graph went higher. The peak also shifted toward higher frequencies as the temperature rose, corresponding to the changing color that the experimenters could observe. But no matter how high the temperature, the measured intensity always rose to a peak and then dropped off sharply at higher frequencies.

Planck developed a mathematical model of a hot, radiating body as a collection of vibrating atoms, each producing electromagnetic waves. The sum of those waves produced a calculated spectrum, which he graphed. His method produced a remarkable match to actual data at the low-frequency end, but it failed miserably in the ultraviolet region. Instead of reaching a peak and then dropping off, Planck's model produced an ever-rising light intensity at high frequencies—which has been called an **"ultraviolet catastrophe"**—for his model.

Then Planck hit on a mathematical trick. His original model allowed each atomic vibration to have any amount of energy, no matter how small, as if energy were a liquid that you could measure out in any amount. Planck replaced that model with one in which energy came in discrete bits like grains of sand. He called the unit of energy a "quantum." The vibrations could carry zero, one, two, or three quanta of energy, and so forth. But they could not have anything in between those whole numbers, such as a third of a quantum or two and one-half quanta.

Planck realized that if the quanta were small, they wouldn't affect his results much. You can measure out almost exactly any volume of very fine sand that you'd like. But if the quanta were large, like a pile of pebbles instead of fine sand, then many of the energy values possible in his original model could not be achieved in the new one. If he had fine grains at low frequencies and large grains at high frequencies, he could eliminate the "ultraviolet catastrophe." To make that happen, Planck kept the ratio between the quantum's energy and frequency the same. If the frequency was twice as large, the quantum had to be twice as big. Triple the frequency, and the quantum's energy also tripled, and so on.

The "ultraviolet catastrophe" disappeared. By adjusting the ratio, Planck was able to make the peaks of his graphs match the peaks from actual experiments. But that was not all. Astonishingly, there was one special ratio that made the calculated intensity match the measured values not just at the peaks but also at all frequencies and all temperatures. That special ratio became known as Planck's constant.

Planck published his results in 1900. He knew that his mathematical trick and the ratio he had discovered were trying to tell him something about physics, but he didn't understand the message.

Planck's Quanta and Photoelectricity

Ultraviolet light also played a role in another puzzling phenomenon. When J. J. Thomson spoke of finding electrons in many circumstances in his 1906 Nobel Prize lecture, he included the photoelectric effect, in which a beam of light could knock electrons out of certain metals. To release electrons, each metal has a particular "threshold" frequency. Below that frequency, the metal does not give up its electrons, no matter how intense, or bright, the light. Above that frequency, even the dimmest light would free some electrons. For most metals, that threshold was in the violet or ultraviolet range. But why should there be a threshold frequency at all?

The threshold question was answered in a paper written in 1905 by a little-known patent clerk in Switzerland named Albert Einstein (1879–1955). Einstein knew that the amount of energy needed to free an electron varied from one metal to another. He realized that if Planck's quanta were not merely mathematical conveniences but real particles, they might be responsible for the photoelectric threshold. Einstein explained that light quanta (later called **photons**) do not gang up like individuals on a tug-of-war team to apply a greater push. Either a photon has enough energy to knock out an electron all by itself, or the electron stays put.

A hot body glows in all wavelengths, producing a continuous spectrum. However, excited atoms produce line spectra that are particular to that element, such as this one for hydrogen. Niels Bohr's atomic theory explained that line spectra resulted when electrons moved from one allowed **energy level** to a lower one. The difference in energy shows up as a quantum of a particular wavelength of light.

Photons below the frequency threshold simply lack the energy needed to knock electrons free, no matter how many there are. Above the frequency threshold, even a single photon has enough energy to free an electron, so even the dimmest light of that color can free electrons.

Light: Waves, Particles, or Both?

Thanks to Young's experiment, everyone had been convinced that light was not a stream of particles, but a series of waves. Maxwell's equations had even identified the waves as electromagnetic. The case seemed closed, but Einstein's work was calling for a new trial. Now light seemed to be made of waves in some circumstances and particles in others! How could that be?

The first steps toward an answer came from Danish physicist Niels Bohr (1885–1962), who was looking for a solution to Rutherford's unstable planetary model of the atom, and had begun to study the spectra of electrically excited gases. These gases had very different spectra from the continuous bands of color produced by a hot furnace. When the light from such gases was spread into a spectrum, each gas produced a distinct series of bright lines. The glowing gas radiated at certain frequencies but not others. The hydrogen spectrum in particular had a few sets of frequencies that fit recognizable mathematical relationships.

Bohr made some shrewd guesses about electrons in atoms, which he hoped would provide insight into the spectra. He proposed that nature allowed electrons in atoms to have only certain natural orbits in which they can move without

Einstein's Miracle Year

Physicists often refer to the year 1905 as Einstein's Miracle Year. His paper explaining the photoelectric effect was only one of his three scientific breakthroughs that year. His most famous publication of that year is his theory of special relativity. That work, among other things, showed that mass and energy were two sides of the same coin, related by the famous formula $E=mc^2$. ("Special" refers to the fact that it applies to objects moving at a constant speed relative to one another. Einstein's general theory of relativity, which includes gravity and acceleration, came more than ten years later.)

Einstein's third major publication that year explained the phenomenon known as Brownian motion. If you look closely at pollen grains in water, as Robert Brown (1773–1858) did in 1827, or dust particles in the air, you can see them following a jerky path. Einstein realized that could be explained by random collisions with air or water molecules. Although the molecules are too small to be seen, Brownian motion is direct evidence that they are real.

All three papers were great breakthroughs, and Einstein was awarded the 1921 Nobel Prize in Physics. The award was not for his work in relativity—although that had made him famous outside of physics—but for his understanding the photoelectric effect, which launched the field of quantum mechanics.

Albert Einstein in his "miracle year" of 1905.

radiating. It was as if the planets of the solar system could orbit only at certain specific distances from the sun and nowhere in between.

Using Maxwell's equations and Newton's laws of motion, he was able to compute the ratio of the electron's energy to its frequency of rotation in those orbits. In the allowed orbits, that ratio was a whole number multiple of Planck's constant. No other orbits could exist. When an electron drops from one of those natural orbits to another with lower energy, the energy difference appears as a quantum.

Bohr calculated the frequencies of light that would result from hydrogen's natural orbits, and the results matched the observed lines in the hydrogen spectrum. Other physicists, most notably Arnold Sommerfeld (1868–1951), extended Bohr's work beyond circular orbits to include elliptical ones, like those of the actual planets in the solar system.

The remarkable insights of Bohr and the others led in unexpected directions. For centuries, scientists had asked whether light was made of waves or particles. They never imagined that the answer could be both, or that they would have to abandon the sharp distinction between particles and waves altogether.

3 HOW
Electrons Explain Chemistry

I f light, long to be thought of as a wave phenomenon, could sometimes behave like a stream of particles, could particles such as electrons sometimes behave like waves? In 1924, a French physics student named Louis-Victor de Broglie (1892–1987) explored that question in his doctoral dissertation. His answer was a clear yes. He devised a formula that used Planck's constant to relate an electron's wavelength to its speed, and he discovered that the circumference of the allowed orbits in Bohr's theory was a whole number of electron wavelengths.

Now the distinction between particles and waves had blurred completely, and other physicists struggled to find new ways to understand the laws of motion within the atom. Among them was Erwin Schrödinger (1887–1961), who developed an equation that described a particle's position by a mathematical formula called a **wave function**. Schrödinger's equation launched a new field of physics called quantum mechanics. Strangely, a particle was no longer considered to be in an

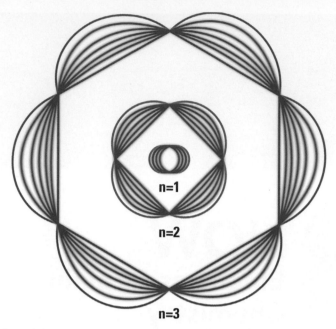

n=1

n=2

n=3

In his 1924 doctoral dissertation, Louis de Broglie launched a new approach to quantum mechanics by extending Planck's idea that light had both wavelike and particle-like properties to electrons. In Bohr's model of the atom, electrons could orbit in certain allowed energy levels. De Broglie replaced that with electrons as waves wrapped around a nucleus. The circumference of the allowed orbits was a whole number of electron wavelengths.

exact place. Rather, the particle's wave function gave the probability of finding it in many different places.

To understand what that means, imagine an object bouncing back and forth so fast on a very tight spring that all you can see is a blur. Near the ends of its bounces, the object moves more slowly and the blurriness decreases. So where is the object? It could be anywhere along the path, but it is more likely to be near one of the less blurry ends than in the blurry middle. In quantum mechanics, the blur is the object.

When Schrödinger applied his equation to the hydrogen atom, it produced a series of different electron wave functions, each concentrated at a certain distance from the nucleus and each had a certain energy. The distances, orbital shapes, and energies were the same ones that Bohr, Sommerfeld, and de Broglie had calculated.

How Large Is an Atom?

Quantum mechanics provides the answer to many puzzling aspects of the subatomic world. For example, it helps explain how, if the nucleus is so small and electrons have so little mass, an atom can be so much larger than the nucleus. The answer is that you can't simply think of an electron as a tiny particle following an orbit; you have to consider its wavelike properties as suggested by Louis de Broglie. Instead of being in a particular spot on the orbit, its wave function means that it is everywhere in that orbit all the time.

As you will read later in this chapter, each electron in an atom is in a different orbit. The size of the atom is therefore the size of the largest orbit that has an electron.

Louis de Broglie in 1929, the year he won the Nobel Prize

PERIODIC TABLE OF

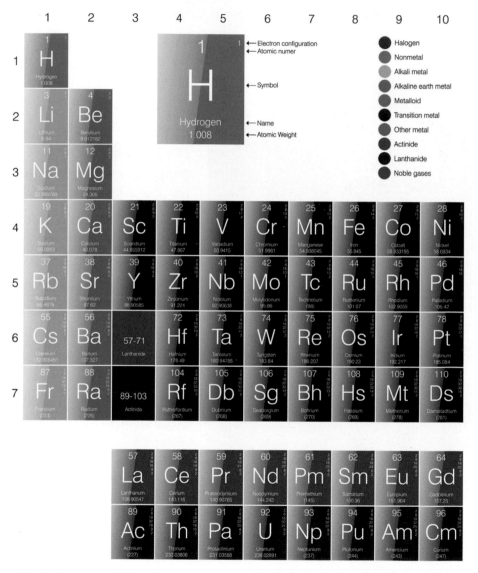

The Modern Periodic Table includes many elements that were undiscovered when Mendeleyev first proposed it. It also reverses the roles of rows and columns from Mendeleyev's original arrangement.

THE ELEMENTS

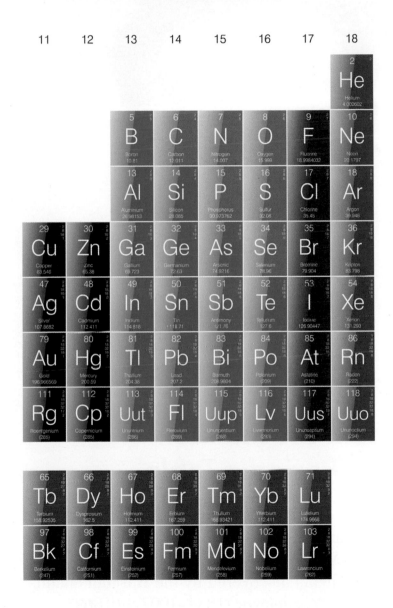

Building on an idea of Louis de Broglie that electrons and other particles have wavelike properties, Erwin Schrödinger devised an equation that represented particles as "wave functions" that change in space and time.

Quantum Mechanics and the Periodic Table

As physicists looked more deeply, they discovered that quantum mechanics could also explain one of chemistry's great mysteries. What underlies the regularity of the periodic table of the elements discovered by the Russian chemist Dmitry Ivanovich Mendeleyev (1834–1907) in 1869?

Mendeleyev had arranged the known elements by increasing atomic weight into columns and then rows. Modern periodic

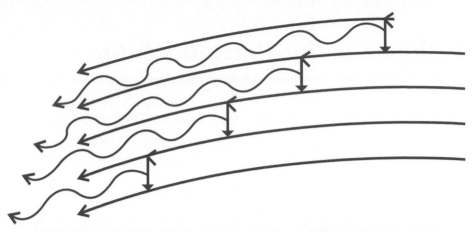

Quantum Jumps. As quantum mechanics evolved, energy levels and electron wave functions replaced Rutherford's idea of orbiting electrons. Bohr's model of the atom, in which electrons make quantum jumps between energy levels and emit quanta of light, explained the observed line spectra of various elements. It also removed Rutherford's concern that orbiting electrons would radiate energy and spiral into the nucleus.

tables order the elements by rows and then columns. All the elements in one of Mendeleyev's rows formed similar compounds. In today's table, the properties are similar down a column.

For example, sodium is above potassium in column I, and both form chloride molecules with one atom of chlorine. Their neighboring atoms in column II—magnesium and calcium—form chloride molecules containing two chlorine atoms. After the electron was discovered, it soon became apparent that the different number of electrons in atoms determined their placement in Mendeleyev's columns. It took quantum mechanics to reveal the explanation.

In quantum theory, each electron orbit in an atom can be labeled by a set of quantum numbers. The principal quantum number, called n, is equal to the number of electron wavelengths that fit into that orbit. The electron's "orbital" quantum number, denoted by the letter l, describes how elliptical the orbit can be. The value of l must always be less than the principal quantum number n. Thus when n is one, l must be zero (a circular orbit). When n equals two, l may be zero or one.

Filling Up the Periodic Table

Mendeleyev's original periodic table was different from the modern periodic table in significant ways. In Mendeleyev's time, chemists were able to measure the atomic weight of elements, but they were not aware of electrons or the nucleus. Modern chemists know

Mendeleyev first conceived the periodic table of the elements in 1859.

about the atomic number, which is the positive electric charge of an element's nucleus. That number corresponds to the number of electrons when the atom is in its electrically neutral state.

Mendeleyev ordered the elements down columns and then across rows by increasing atomic weight. The modern periodic table orders the elements across rows and then down columns by increasing atomic number. Usually an element with a larger atomic number also has a larger atomic weight, but there are a few exceptions. So besides the reversed role of rows and columns, the order of elements is slightly different today than in Mendeleyev's time.

The most important difference between the tables is the gaps in Mendeleyev's table where elements had not yet been discovered. In order to group elements with similar properties across his rows, Mendeleyev left blank spaces. He predicted that elements would be found to fill in those spaces, and he described their properties. When they were later discovered, it was a great triumph for his idea.

Mendeleyev left out an entire group of elements, which are known today as the noble gases. Those elements—helium, neon, argon, krypton, xenon, and radon—have no **valence electrons** and thus do not react chemically without a lot of added energy. Sir William Ramsay (1852–1916) and Lord Rayleigh—whose insistence that J. J. Thomson do experimental work led to Thomson's discovery of the electron—were the first to discover these gases.

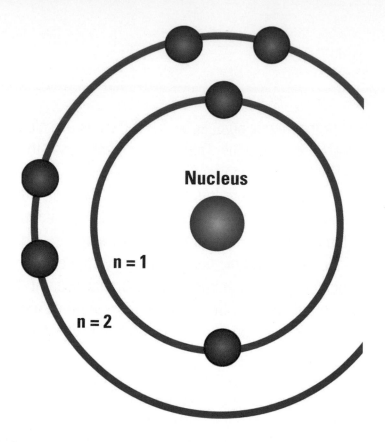

A third quantum number, called *m* for magnetic, envisions the nucleus as a sphere with a north-south axis. An electron's orbital plane can go around the equator (*m*=0), or it can be tilted a different amount, corresponding to the value of m. The value of *m* is less than or equal to the value of *l*. And m can have either a positive or negative sign, depending on whether its orbital direction is clockwise or counterclockwise.

Finally, just as Earth spins on its axis once per day while orbiting the Sun once a year, an electron also has a spin quantum number, denoted by *s*, which can only be in one of two states, often called spin up (*s*=+1/2) and spin down (*s*=−1/2). No two electrons in the same atom can have the same "quantum state," or the same set of values for *n*, *l*, *m*, and *s*. Physicists discovered that electrons would fill the quantum

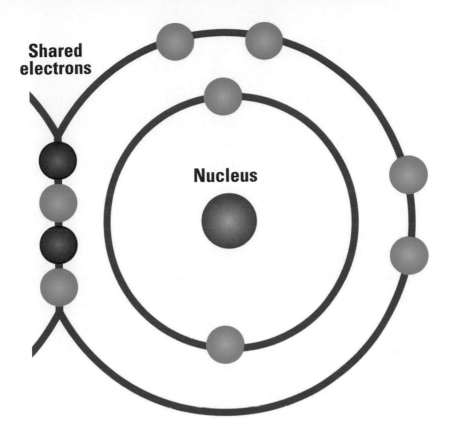

Shared electrons

Nucleus

Molecules are formed when two or more atoms bond together, usually in a way that fills an electronic shell or subshell. One way to do that is through sharing electrons in a covalent bond. For example, two oxygen atoms bond covalently to form an oxygen molecule. Each atom's outer shell has six electrons, two short of the eight needed to complete that shell. Two oxygen atoms bond when each shares two of its outer electrons with the other, completing the outer shells of both.

states in a predictable order. Some electron arrangements were especially favorable. Those are the noble gases (see Filling Up the Periodic Table on pages 40–41), and larger atoms would build up from those as a core.

Atoms in the same column of the periodic table have the same pattern of electrons in their outer orbits around different cores. Those outside electrons, called valence electrons, are responsible for an atom's chemical behavior. Quantum mechanics explained why the periodic table is periodic!

Chemical Bonds

Once that explanation was known, physicists and chemists began speaking of electrons filling "**shells**," which were sets of all the quantum states having the same value of n, or "subshells," which were smaller parts of those shells having certain values of l and m. In any column of the periodic table, the core electrons were always in completely filled inner shells and subshells, and the valence electrons were in partially filled outer subshells.

The fewer valence electrons there are, the easier it is to remove them. The elements in column I of the periodic table, sodium and potassium, for example, have only one valence electron, which they give up easily. On the opposite side of the periodic table, the valence electrons are close to filling a subshell, and thus have greater attraction not only for each other but also for other electrons that may be nearby. Fluorine and chlorine in column VII, for example, need only one more electron to complete a subshell.

When a chlorine atom and a sodium atom get close to each other, the chlorine snatches the sodium's valence electron, leaving both as electrically charged "ions" with filled subshells. The positively charged sodium ion and the negatively charged chloride ion experience a strong electrical attraction—an **ionic bond**—that results in a sodium chloride molecule.

Other kinds of atoms, especially those in the center columns of the periodic table, may join together by sharing rather than exchanging electrons. That is called **covalent bonding**. For example, a nitrogen atom has three valence electrons in a subshell that can hold six. When two nitrogen atoms share all their valence electrons in a covalent triple bond, it completes the subshells of both. The result is a two-atom nitrogen molecule. Oxygen atoms too, with four of six possible electrons in their outer subshells, share two valence electrons each in a covalent double bond to form two-atom oxygen molecules.

Metals get their special properties from a different type of chemical bonding. Each atom shares all of its outer electrons with every other atom, so the **metallic bonds** are not between pairs of atoms but rather between each atom and the whole. As a result, those shared electrons are bound only weakly to their nearest atom and flow easily to the next one, explaining why metals carry electricity so well. The shared electrons are thus often called "conduction electrons."

Metallic bonding is also involved in both the photoelectric effect and cathode rays. If a strip of metal is placed in a beam of ultraviolet light, each photon carries enough energy to free a conduction electron. Likewise, the electric field in a vacuum tube is strong enough to pull some conduction electrons from a metal cathode.

In a way, all of chemistry is the study of electrons—from the periodic table to understanding how atoms bond with each other through sharing or exchange of electrons. That is also true of much of modern technology. Understanding how to control electrons has led to an array of electronic devices that are changing the way people live, work, and communicate no matter where in the world they live.

4 ELECTRONIC Technology

I n 1934, thirty-seven years after his discovery of the electron, J. J. Thomson spoke of its importance in technology. "Now the electron has come into commerce," he noted, "and large workshops and many thousands of workers are employed in its production." He was especially thinking about radio communication. If he were alive today, he would be astonished at the many technologies that have developed from his discovery.

Even though commercial radio was less than fifteen years old at that time, it had already transformed the world. Radios of that time were four-foot- (1.2-meter) high cabinets filled with wires and vacuum tubes. Some tubes were as large as today's 12-ounce (29.6-milliliter) soft drink cans. Inside the tubes were two or more electrodes, including a cathode, a heated filament like the one in a light bulb. The heat freed conduction electrons, which would flow toward the **anode** like balls rolling downhill. The greater the voltage is, the steeper the hill, and the faster the flow of electric current.

The shape of the other electrodes and their voltage levels would affect that current flow. Small changes in voltage could produce large changes in the current flow through the tube. In that way, the tubes could be used as amplifiers. Passing radio waves would create a weak electric signal in the antenna. The tubes could amplify that signal to power electromagnets, which in turn made smaller magnets vibrate inside cone speakers, made from paper, producing sound.

Tubes could also act as controllable on-off switches or one-way flow valves for electric currents. Those uses turned out to be ideal for computing, where information of all kinds can be represented in a binary code made up of zeroes and ones. By the 1950s, improvements in electronics reduced radios to the size of shoeboxes, and a few companies had begun to make room-size computers for the military and a few large corporations.

From Tubes to Microchips

Then in the 1950s came a breakthrough—the transistor, a device that took advantage of the way electrons move in materials called semiconductors, such as silicon. Silicon atoms have four valence electrons, and they join together in a regular arrangement called a crystal by sharing one valence electron with each of four neighboring silicon atoms to fill an eight-electron subshell. Since they are shared among several atoms, the valence electrons can flow easily, but not like in a metal. Atoms are always jiggling, so a few electrons come free. Each free electron leaves behind a "hole," which readily accepts a new electron. If you could look inside a semiconductor

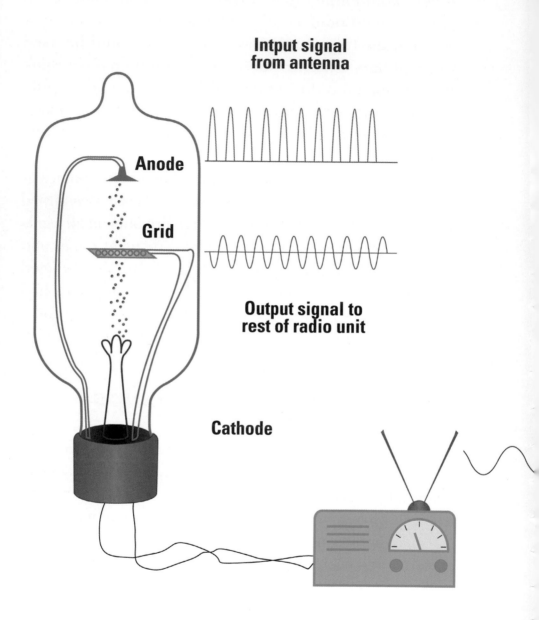

**Intput signal
from antenna**

Anode

Grid

**Output signal to
rest of radio unit**

Cathode

Many early radios used vacuum tubes to either transform an incoming radio signal into an electric current or make that electric current stronger. This triode is a cathode ray tube with a grid between the heated cathode that produces electrons and an anode that receives them. A negative charge on the grid reduces the flow of electrons, while a positive charge enhances it. The charge on the grid follows the pattern of the radio signal, producing a similar pattern in the current through the triode.

connected to a battery, you would see electrons moving from the negative end to the positive end, and "holes" moving in the opposite direction.

To turn a piece of silicon into a transistor, scientists "dope" it by adding small amounts other substances whose atoms replace silicon atoms in the crystal. If the additive has five valence electrons like phosphorus, the silicon has extra negatively charged electrons and is called an "n-type." Adding a substance that has only three valence electrons like aluminum results in "p-type" material with an excess of positively charged holes. The first transistors were n-type and p-type semiconductors joined in a sandwich arrangement. The layers of the sandwich affect electric currents in the same ways as the electrodes in vacuum tubes. Semiconductor devices, however, use much less power, operate much faster, and are also much smaller and cheaper.

By the 1960s, transistor radios were everywhere and computers were becoming more common. But another breakthrough was in the works. Instead of making transistors one at a time, scientists and engineers devised ways to make hundreds, then thousands, on a single sliver of silicon,

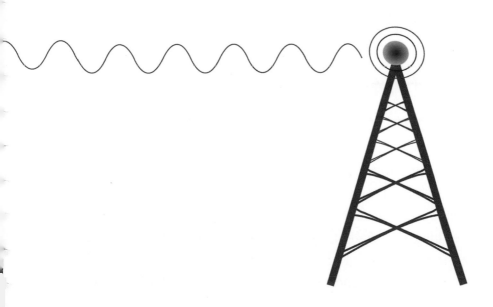

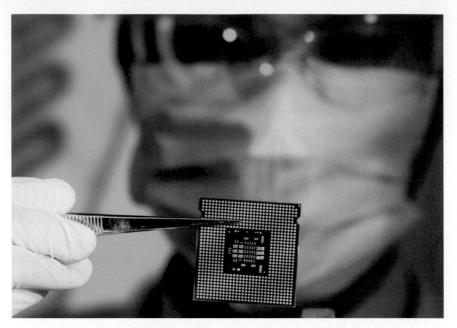

Modern integrated circuits, such as this microprocessor chip, contain tens of millions of interconnected transistors in an area the size of a human thumbnail. This has led to advanced electronic communications and computing technology, such as tablet computers and cell phones, and televisions small enough to wear on your wrist.

connected into integrated circuits, commonly called "chips" or "microchips." Today, computer chips with many millions of transistors are everywhere, and companies are continuing to find ways to pack more circuitry into less material for less cost.

Magnifying with Electron Waves

Though the quantum world has oddities such as fuzzy, wavelike electrons, scientists have learned to take advantage of quantum phenomena to explore very small objects. Microscopes cannot produce images of objects smaller than the wavelength of the energy they are using. For example, the wavelength of visible light is smaller than bacteria, but much larger than viruses.

Yet you have probably seen images of viruses. Those images were created by **electron microscopes**.

Electron microscopes are possible because high-energy electrons have very short wavelengths, and magnets can bend their paths. Scientists have constructed electron microscopes with magnetic lenses and use them to study not only viruses, but also new "high-tech" materials.

Transistors on integrated circuits are constantly decreasing in size, and the same is true of many other useful structures. People working in the important fields of materials science

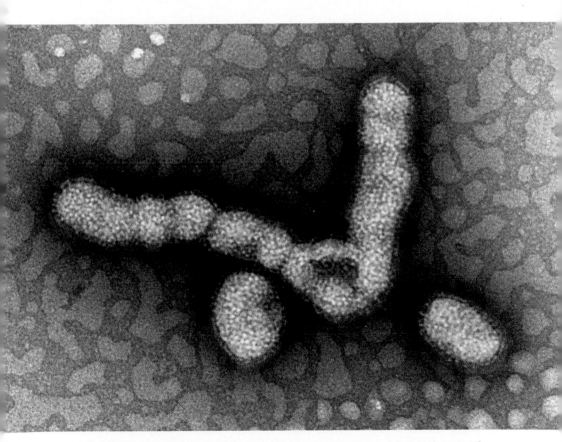

This image produced by an electron microscope shows a few viruses of the type that caused a worldwide outbreak of the disease commonly called the swine flu in 2009. Unlike bacteria, most viruses are much smaller than the wavelength of visible light and thus can't be imaged in an ordinary light microscope. Electron wavelengths are about the size of atoms and enable scientists to study viruses in detail.

"Seeing" Atoms

The wavelike nature of electrons even makes it possible for scientists to observe individual atoms or molecules with devices called scanning **tunneling** microscopes (STMs) and atomic force microscopes (AFMs). Both devices use a small sharp needle that moves just above the surface being measured. The needle is so close to the surface that the wave functions of electrons at its tip extend into the material. That means that each electron has a small probability of crossing the gap as part of a "tunneling" current, so named because the electrons seem to tunnel through an energy barrier rather than go over it. By scanning the needle back and forth across the surface, an STM produces an image of the atoms on the surface from the varying intensity of the tunneling current.

An AFM keeps the tunneling current constant by allowing the needle to move up and down on a spring-like device as it scans the surface. In effect, it "feels" the surface bumps as it moves along. Scientists are now finding ways to pick up and move single atoms or molecules using devices such as AFMs.

and materials engineering need to be able to check out how the chemistry and structure of those materials varies from place to place. Electron microscopes not only produce images, but they also create X-rays that can be used to identify the atoms in the tiny regions that the electrons hit.

Another kind of imaging uses a different kind of electron. You may have read or heard about antimatter, especially if you're a fan of science fiction. But antimatter is real. Every subatomic particle has its antiparticle with the same mass but an opposite charge. If the two particles meet, they annihilate

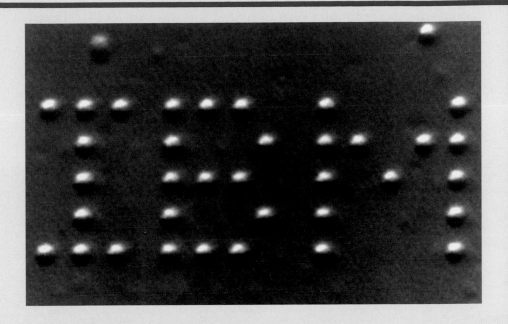

The quantum mechanical phenomenon called tunneling has led to the development of instruments that can detect and move individual atoms, as illustrated by this image from the IBM corporation of its name formed by atoms of a different element placed on a silicon background.

each other, producing two very energetic photons (gamma rays) going in opposite directions.

The electron's antiparticle is the **positron**. Just as many radioactive elements produce beta rays, which are really electrons, a few produce positrons. A medical device called a positron emission tomography (PET) scanner produces images of the living brain that identify brain damage and abnormalities better than any other technique. Materials scientists use positron beams to identify microscopic defects in metallic crystal structures that signal the very earliest signs of metal fatigue.

J. J. Thomson could never imagine that electronics would lead to such wonders. But he knew that the road to the future often begins in the laboratory. "Any new discovery contains the germ of a new industry," he said in 1934. "Take the hair of the dog that bit you, and go in for more and more research." As anyone who follows advances in communications, computing, and other modern technologies knows, Thomson could hardly be accused of barking up the wrong tree.

We live in an electronic age where personal computers are everywhere and everyday devices from microwave ovens and toasters to cars and traffic signals contain microprocessors. This has brought many changes in our homes and in the way we interact with each other.

Glossary

atom The smallest bit of matter than can be identified as a certain chemical element.

anode and cathode The positive and negative terminals of a battery or pieces of metal (electrodes) attached to them.

cathode ray A beam of electrons that flows from the cathode in a glass tube from which most of the air has been removed.

compound A substance made of only one kind of molecule that consists of more than one kind of atom. For example, water is made of molecules that contain two atoms of hydrogen and one atom of oxygen.

covalent, ionic, and metallic bonds Different ways in which atoms can join together by sharing or exchanging some of their electrons.

electromagnetic wave A form of energy resulting from the interrelationship of changing electric and magnetic fields that flows through space at the speed of light.

electromagnetism A fundamental force of nature, or property of matter and energy, that includes electricity, magnetism, and electromagnetic waves, such as light.

electrometer Any of various instruments for measuring electric charge or electrical potential difference.

electronics A field of technology that takes advantage of the ability to control the motion of electrons.

electron microscope A technology that uses the wavelike or quantum mechanical properties of electrons to produce images of very small objects or features.

element A substance made of only one kind of atom.

energy level One of many values of energy that an electron can have in an atom.

molecule The smallest bit of matter that can be identified as a certain chemical compound.

photon A particle that carries electromagnetic energy, such as light energy.

positron The antiparticle of an electron. If an electron and positron meet, they annihilate each other and produce pure energy in the form of two high-energy photons traveling in opposite directions.

quantum mechanics A field of physics developed to describe the relationships between matter and energy that accounts for the dual wave-particle nature of both.

shells and subshells Particularly stable sets of energy levels in atoms that electrons tend to occupy.

spectrum The mixture of colors contained within a beam of light, or the band produced when those colors are spread out by a prism or other device that separates the colors from each other.

tunneling A quantum mechanical phenomenon in which, due to its wavelike properties, a particle crosses a barrier, as if through a tunnel, when it lacks sufficient energy to get over the top.

ultraviolet catastrophe A breakdown in Max Planck's mathematical description of the spectrum of hot bodies that required him to devise the idea of the quantum.

valence electron One of the electrons outside an atom's filled shells or subshells. Valence electrons are responsible for the atom's chemical properties.

wave function The quantum mechanical description that expresses the wavelike properties of a particle.

For Further Information

Books

Bortz, Fred. *Physics: Decade by Decade*. Twentieth-Century Science. New York: Facts On File, 2007.

———. *Laws of Motion and Isaac Newton*. New York: Rosen, 2014.

———. *The Periodic Table of Elements and Dmitry Mendeleev*. New York: Rosen, 2014.

Hollar, Sherman. *Electronics*. New York: Britannica Educational Services, 2012.

Marsico, Katie. *Key Discoveries in Physical Science*. Minneapolis, MN: Lerner Publications, 2015.

Winterberg, Jenna. *Electromagnetism*. Huntington Beach, CA: Teacher Created Materials, 2015.

Websites

American Institute of Physics Center for the History of Physics

www.aip.org/history-programs/physics-history

This site includes several valuable online exhibits from the history of physics, including The Discovery of the Electron and Rutherford's Nuclear World.

The Nobel Foundation Prizes for Physics

www.nobelprize.org/nobel_prizes/physics

Read about past Nobel Prize winners, including J. J. Thomson, Ernest Rutherford, Louis de Broglie, Albert Einstein, and George Paget Thomson (1892–1975). Each entry includes quick biographical facts and brief summaries of their award-winning contributions to physics.

The Science Museum (UK)

www.sciencemuseum.org.uk

This site includes the online exhibit Atomic Firsts, which tells the story of J. J. Thomson, Ernest Rutherford, and Thomson's son George Paget Thomson, who also won the Nobel Prize for his experiment that proved the existence of de Broglie's predicted electron waves.

Museums and Institutes

American Institute of Physics
Center for the History of Physics
One Physics Ellipse
College Park, MD 20740
(301) 209-3165
www.aip.org/history-programs/physics-history

The Center for History of Physics houses a research library, a photo archive, and has created numerous online resources in all areas of physics, including The Discovery of the Electron (aip.org/history/electron/jjhome.htm) and Rutherford's Nuclear World (aip.org/history/exhibits/rutherford).

Institute of Electrical and Electronics Engineers
3 Park Avenue, 17th Floor
New York, NY 10016-5997
(212) 419-7900
www.ieee.org

The IEEE, pronounced "Eye-triple-E," is the world's largest professional association dedicated to advancing technological innovation and excellence for the benefit of humanity. In the engineering and scientific community, it is best known for its highly cited publications, conferences, technology standards, and professional and educational activities.

Lederman Science Education Center
Fermilab MS 777
Box 500
Batavia, IL 60510
(630) 840-8258
ed.fnal.gov/lsc/lscvideo/index.shtml

This museum is an outstanding place to discover the science and history of subatomic particles. It is located at the Fermi National Accelerator Laboratory (Fermilab) outside of Chicago.

National Electronics Museum
1745 West Nursery Road
Linthicum, MD 21090
(410) 765-0230
www.nationalelectronicsmuseum.org

This museum's exhibits tell the story of the United States' defense electronics industry. From telegraph and radio to radar and satellites, it offers visitors access to the electronic marvels that have helped to shape the United States and our world.

Ontario Science Centre
770 Don Mills Road
Toronto, Ontario M3C 1T3
Canada
(416) 696-1000
www.ontariosciencecentre.ca

The Ontario Science Centre is Canada's leading science and technology museum. Its programs and exhibits aim to inspire a lifelong journey of curiosity, discovery, and action to create a better future for the planet.

Index

Page numbers in **boldface** are illustrations. Entries in **boldface** are glossary terms.

About the Authors

Science educator and consultant **B. H. Fields** has worked behind the scenes in the publishing industry since the mid-1980s, specializing in books and articles on the physical sciences and technology for middle grades.

Award-winning children's author **Fred Bortz** spent the first twenty-five years of his working career as a physicist, gaining experience in fields as varied as nuclear reactor design, automobile engine control systems, and science education. He earned his PhD at Carnegie Mellon University, where he also worked in several research groups from 1979 through 1994. He has been a full-time writer since 1996.